Angels I Have Seen

Rev. Marcia Cope Fleischman

ARPress
ILLUMINATING IDEAS,
EMPOWERING VOICES

ARPress LLC
45 Dan Road Suite 5
Canton MA 02021
Hotline: 1(888) 821-0229
Fax: 1(508) 545-7580

Ordering Information:
Quantity sales. Special discounts are available on quantity purchases by corporations, associations, and others. For details, contact the publisher at the address above.

Printed in the United States of America.

ISBN-13:   Softcover   979-8-89330-500-5
            eBook   979-8-89330-501-2

Library of Congress Control Number: 2024900442

"For He will give
His angels charge
Concerning you.
To guard you in all your ways.
They will lift you up
In their hands,
So that you will not
Strike
Your foot upon
A
Stone."

(Luke 4:10-11)

Dedication

This book is dedicated to my

Lung donor,

Andrew Thomas Arnold

And to his father and sister,

Jack Arnold and Shawna Arnold Scott.

Who saved my life.

And to my best friend,

Ken Fleischman.

Who sustains my life.

An Amazing Mystical Journey Begins

"There is no such thing as old visions of angels. I will give you new visions of angels to paint!"

The message from the Spirit had come loud and clear, at least it was clear.

The Spirit's voice is seldom loud. In fact it is not even audible. The voice was one that I had learned to hear speaking since 1983. It has been an amazing journey since my first real mystical vision. The inner journey is my passion, this journey with the Spirit of God.

Jesus said to his disciples, "I have more to tell you but you cannot hear it now. When the Spirit of truth comes, He will remind you of all I have said to you and will lead you into all truth. (John 14:23)

We are designed to communicate with God through the Holy Spirit that lives in us…the divine Spirit that is the same as the individual spirit that is our eternal being. We are created to receive messages from the Spirit of God. It just takes some practice and a spiritual community that teaches:

1. that it is possible to hear and see messages from the Spirit and

2. that encourages us to strengthen our abilities to hear and see.

This is the kind of church I have been part of for most of my adult life….where I opened up spiritually, where my mystical gifts began and were encouraged. I have been looking for more of God all of my life and this is where and how I found it.

God started speaking to me in inner words that "sound" like me talking to myself, but I began to recognize the "voice" is not my own. The message is received rather that self-generated.

Seeing Picture Messages from the Spirit

One day during church service the Spirit began to speak to me in picture messages. I heard many people talk about the pictures that came to their minds while praying. The effect of hearing about these experiences was like throwing gasoline on a fire. It ignited my spirit and I wanted that experience for myself. My desire was answered.

The first picture I saw from the Spirit was a picture of Jesus with children.

I had our youngest daughter sitting on my lap during the worship service. Sarah was two years old and a bit of a wiggle worm. She usually was in the nursery during church but for some reason this day she was with me.

I thought "Brother, I am not going to hear anything from the Spirit today during quiet time!" I usually sat very still listening for a brief word from God. Because of Sarah's energy I knew I would be too distracted to hear a thing in that quiet internal place. But I closed my eyes to concentrate and listen anyway. BAM, a picture popped into my mind.

This "picture" was of Jesus standing in the middle of a big group of rowdy children. He was at least two feet taller than any of the children. The children were pushing and shoving and running around yelling and laughing. They were having fun. And Jesus was standing in the middle of it all laughing and laughing. Wow!

What was the message of this brief "video picture"? It was that Jesus was enjoying all of this kid energy and so could I. God was inviting me to enjoy Sarah's energy and not be irritated by it. And God was showing me that I could "hear" Him speak in the middle of the madness…..in fact, I could "see" visions in the middle of the madness, too. Wow! This was amazing!

I began to realize that I am a "visual" person. I slowly became awake to this part of me. The Spirit of God, whom I sought with all my inner being, responded to my longing, longing for more of Him. The inner hunger for more of God became fulfilled with the release of the Spirit within me.

I found that the images coming to my mind were most active, first, when I was in worship where the Presence of God was strongest and, second, when I was praying, hands on, for people at church. We pray a lot for people. We even have healing prayer times built into the worship service so we can pray for people. We have a prayer meeting once a month so we can pray for people and listen to what the Spirit is saying to them. During these early experiences of praying for others I would receive picture messages for the person receiving prayer.

For a long time I was too shy to tell people what I was "seeing" for them as I prayed silently for them. I would just find myself extremely blessed and amused by what I was "seeing." Then, one day as I was praying the Spirit said to me "Marcia, I am not giving you these pictures for your own amusement. I am giving them for you to share with the people." These picture messages or visions are a gift that is meant for the healing of the one receiving prayer. I hesitatingly began to share what I was seeing.

"I think I am seeing a picture for you. If it speaks to you about your life, keep it. If it doesn't fit, just let it go." I would say to the person receiving prayer. A person must always be empowered to receive or reject the message. I know I do not always hear purely what is from the Spirit. Discernment is always important. A true message from the Spirit always feels like love. This is the discerning method. Does this image or word from the Spirit feel like love? If it does not, it is not from God. More and more often the person receiving the message, in picture or word would exclaim that the "image" was just what she/he needed to hear.

For example, one time I shared a picture with someone who had just moved from out of town. We were having a healing prayer service at church and he came forward to receive prayer... He didn't say anything. We just began to pray silently and "listen" to what the Spirit was revealing. I saw a picture of this person hiding in a box. It was dark in there. Jesus was sitting there with him. As I "watched" this scene, I told him what I saw. I continued reporting what I was seeing in the picture. He was sitting in this big box with Jesus. When he began to trust Jesus he opened a drawer in the bottom of the box where he had jewels hidden. He started to show the jewels to Jesus. When I described this picture, he jumped back saying, "How did you know that? How did you know that?"

I said, "How did I know what?"

He then told me that I had seen an image of something from his childhood. As a child his dysfunctional family would get our of control. They were verbally, physically and sexually abusive. He would be scared and would hide in his toy box. To comfort himself, he would pretend that all of the things he loved, his teacher, his friends and his favorite toys were jewels. I had "seen" him showing his "jewels" to Jesus.

How did I know that? Indeed, I didn't know anything about this person. I had only just met him. The Spirit of God had revealed this image to me. God was encouraging this man to trust Jesus. Jesus represents God with skin on. And he was comforting this person in his distress.

By using me, and sending this picture message, God was bringing healing to this man's wounded heart. The Spirit revealed that God had been with this man since he was a child and was there to comfort and heal him.

This "seeing" and "hearing" from the Spirit is the gift of prophecy that the Apostle Paul speaks about in the book of First Corinthians. He tells us all to desire this gift over all the gifts.

Now, I wish I could say that I was bold in claiming this gift and moved out in great confidence in using it for the encouragement and healing of others. But I didn't. I just hesitatingly moved forward trying to offer whatever I could for someone's comfort.

Then, one day, I was in church. I was scheduled to have major surgery the next day. I was scared to death about the surgery, and the Spirit showed me a picture of angels.

Do you believe in angels? Have you ever encountered one? I believe in them and I have seen them in visions and in the "flesh" so to speak... My life has been changed by angels.

Seeing Angels for the First Time

For many years I have been fascinated by angel stories. I did not realize that people really believed in angels. I listened to a tape that I ordered from a Christian Healing Prayer Ministry in Florida. It was filled with angel stories. It was a talk by a woman I respected for her expertise in healing prayer, Judith McNutt. Judith told some amazing stories of people who had seen or experienced the presence of angels and been changed or impacted by these encounters. Up until that time, when I was in my early thirties, I had never considered that angels were real. They were only statues or Christmas ornaments or decorations that referenced the Christmas story of the birth of

Jesus. Of course there was the angel Clarence on the movie "It's A Wonderful Life". I remember Clarence saying, "If people believe in angels, why are they surprised when they see one?"

I joined the church when I was twelve years old. I had finished a year-long class where we learned about faith and church dogma and the Westminster Catechism. I grew up in the First Presbyterian Church of Lexington, Missouri. After finishing the class I made my confession of faith. Even then I knew I was looking for more. It seemed to me that there had to be more to Jesus than attending church once a week for an hour. But what was it?

When I was twenty-one, two of my friends shared that they had a vibrant and exciting encounter with Jesus. Their faith had become real. I wanted to get me some of that! I prayed for Jesus to come into my life. In a new and vibrant way-- BAM... love struck!

Because I was experiencing a life-long mild depression I had never felt loved. I knew I was loved by my family but I never felt loved. When I said "Yes" to Jesus, love broke through my depression. I felt loved for the first time in my life! Everything began to change. I was on the path to becoming a new and different person. I never looked back. Being with God and people who loved God became my passion.

Ten years after I first met Jesus and opened up spiritually I began to hear stories about people encountering angels. I was blown away! Could this be true? Could people in the 20th century be seeing angels ...talking to angels...hearing from angels? I began reading any books I could find about angels. The books that spoke of names and hierarchies never meant much to me. But the stories where people were led by angels, talked to angels, experienced angels, saw angels and heard messages from angles...those were the exciting stories. And with each story I could feel the love of God even more. Could it be that angels are messengers to us from God? I would find out for myself in the not too distant future.

One day, after church, one of the congregation members, I'll call her Jane, called me on the phone. She told me that, while I was preaching, she saw two angels standing beside me, one on either side of me. Jane said that they were very, very tall. Their feet were on the platform and their heads were up by the ceiling above me where it rises up to the dome in the center of the sanctuary. I was speechless. She sensed my reaction and told me that she had been given a gift of seeing angels. She sees them everywhere.

"No," Jane declared, "I haven't been drinking. I just see angels. I just have never seen any as big as the ones standing by you."

Wow! What news! I actually knew someone who saw angels!

As an ordained minister I have been delighted to tell the angel stories to our congregation. These stories fill people with awe just as they do to me.

I learned that Angels are full of light and love. Their purpose is to carry the powerful and delightful love and care of God to us. They most often are depicted as sweet beings with lovely faces and expressions of divine love. My own encounter with angels was both sweet and lovely but also very surprising. One day an angel appeared to me in a form I would never have guessed or chosen. One has to be open to receive the messengers in any form in which they might appear.

Angels appear most often in the middle of life's turmoil.

I was 34 when I started to experience abdominal pain. Soon it became apparent that it was time for a hysterectomy. I had never had major surgery and I was scared. Our neighbor's son-in-law died after surgery from complications with anesthesia. He was only 29 years old. How would I know what would happen? I was scheduled for surgery on the first Monday of December, 1984.

The day before surgery was the first Sunday of Advent and our pastor, Rev. Paul Smith, told some angels stories from a book by Billy Graham. As I was sitting listening an image flashed in my mind, an image of angels. It was a vision, a picture message for me from the Spirit. Usually these visions come to mind during worship or prayer, but always when my eyes are closed. This time I could see the vision but my eyes were open. No, I didn't see them with my eyes, but in the same way I see picture messages. I see them with my spirit on the screen of my mind. It is like seeing a memory in your mind.

I had started having pictures come to my mind while praying in the worship service. They were picture messages from the Holy Spirit. It was the beginning of a gift of seeing that I have enjoyed for many years now. This experience was new back then. I usually sat very quietly with my eyes closed, being open to see some picture from the Spirit. This day was different. I was sitting, listening to the sermon with my eyes wide open when, BAM, an image appeared.

I saw myself lying in my hospital bed sleeping after my surgery. There were angels standing on either side of my bed quietly watching over me. The picture appeared like a pen and ink drawing...just white with black lines. But there were the angels and the effect on me was profound. I relaxed.

I relaxed and let go of my fear. Peace came over me and I was ready to proceed. The surgery went fine. Did I see angels when I woke up from surgery? No. Did I see them at any other time before the surgery? No. But I knew they were there.

The sense of peace never left me.

Although my surgery was the old-fashioned kind with a full incision, I progressed so well in my healing that I went home on Thursday, four days later. All was well.

So that was my first angel encounter. I saw them in a vision. I saw them watching over me. The next encounter would be totally different and amazing.

My mother and mother-in-law were both diagnosed with terminal cancer on the same week in March 1988. We took my father, who had

Alzheimer's to a nursing home the same week. It was an excruciatingly difficult time. My mother was diagnosed with small-cell lung cancer. My mother-in-law had uterine cancer. My mother-in-law died in November of that year. My mother underwent several rounds of chemotherapy and had a few months of rest. The cancer was temporarily at bay. One day I was praying and asking God to keep her from suffering. I heard from the Spirit that she would have a time of peace and then she would deteriorate quickly. God said, "I am calling her to my arms." I wrote this in my prayer journal. I heard that message in the fall as she was selling her home and dividing up her possessions.

Her decline started after the holidays, in the winter of 1989.

I adored my mother. The thought of losing her was almost unbearable. Yet this tragic loss would come to me, as it does to all of us, nonetheless.

During this time of family illnesses I was attending Seminary, driving 25 miles each way from home to school and back. It was a busy time. My mother entered the hospital one last time in March. She loved needlework and was working on a very fine needle point oriental rug for her doll house... now my doll house. As the cancer moved into her bones, she lost the use of her left arm and her legs. She didn't get out of bed again. She worked on her petit point rug by holding it down with her non-functioning left arm and sewing with her right hand. There were no complaints from her.

When I think of courage, I think of my mother. Courage is not standing tall and valiant in the midst of a fight, but, in fear and trembling, taking the next step. My mother was not fearful like me. She had great courage. Bit by bit, after her diagnosis, she began letting go of parts of her life. She knew that the chemotherapy would drain her and that she could no longer care for my dad whose Alzheimer's was slowly taking his mind away. She had us find a nursing home for him.

Mom sold their home and we divided up all of their treasures and gave the rest to a charity auction in town.

The night before we began to go through the house and divide the treasures my sisters and I sat with my mom in the den. We told stories and laughed one last time with the house in tact, the memories flowing and a huge hole in our souls for our father who was not there. When I hear the song "Hold on to the night, Hold on to the memories,"

I can't help but remember that night. We sat holding on to the lifetime that had brought us into being and nurtured us through the years. It was a lifetime that we were saying goodbye to….

letting go of. It was a sad and painful time. But not that night; that night was joy. It is strange how we can carry memories that are still so alive within us.

The doctor's final report was that the cancer had traveled to my mother's brain. She could continue the treatments to buy a little more time, the doctor said. But she was finished with all that. She was ready to continue the journey to the next stage.

Her courage carried her through this tough decision.

"Give me my check book and give me a cigarette," she said. She gave us some money and enjoyed her favorite vice, the one she loved, the one that killed her.

One morning I went to see her and she said, "Marcia, I am ready to go."

I asked her why she said that. She said that someone had been in her room the night before, not a nurse, but someone. They were discussing spiritual things and while they were talking she saw a vision. She saw God's arms reaching down for her. She was ready to go on to the other side.

Next it was time for her to go to the nursing home. Her treatments were over. The doctor estimated that she had 6 to 8 more weeks to live. We got her settled in a wonderful nursing home in the middle of the week on Wednesday.

The next Sunday I saw Harold at church.

Harold is a large African-American man with a very deep voice. He traveled to Kansas City from his home at the Army medical center at Fort Leavenworth, Kansas, to go to church. He had come to Broadway (that is the nickname for our church, Broadway Church) for years. When he visited church he would ask me to give him a ride to his father's home in east Kansas City. I was glad to take him to his father's home. Our two daughters rode in the back seat.

One day I asked Harold why he lived at the Medical center at Fort Leavenworth. He said he had mental problems and a problem with uncontrollable rage. Hummmm. That was a little scary! But Harold was always in control, kind and polite. Later I learned that Harold was scary to some people. He never scared me.

So, it was April 9th and Harold appeared at church. When I entered the sanctuary a little bit late, I saw Harold a few pews down from where I was sitting. He saw me and got up to come sit by me. My husband, Ken, sat on my other side. Now this may not seem unusual, but Harold had never come to sit with me before.

He sat down beside me and said, "How's your mother, Marcia?"

I had not seen Harold for nine months at which time I told him my mother-in-law was dying..

But Harold didn't ask me about her. He asked me about my mother. I said, "She's dying."

Harold replied, "Read these verses."

He pointed out a few verses from the New Testament for me to read. I just wrote down the references, chapters and verses and joined in the worship service.

When we stood to sing, Ken on my left and Harold on my right, I felt like I was surrounded by angels. It was a lovely, sweet feeling of the presence of divine light beings.

That afternoon I stole a few minutes to sit in the living room and look up the verses Harold gave me. This is what they said...

"In the world you will have trouble but I have overcome the world."(John 16:33)

"In my Father's house there are many dwelling places. I go to prepare a place for you." (John 14:2)

"Do not let your hearts be troubled, do not let them be afraid."(John 14:27)

Upon reading these verses I felt a sense of peace penetrate my spirit. My mother died on Tuesday morning, two days later.

My sisters and I were with her when she died. I was holding her hand as she took her last breath.

Suddenly I felt like I was flying. My mother's spirit was passing through me. My sisters left the room to make phone calls but I stayed there, feeling her forehead growing cooler and cooler and holding her hand. With my eyes closed something like a moving scene passed through my mind. I saw my mom flying to the Ash Grove. The Ash Grove is a place in a song. This was one of her favorite Girl Scout songs, *The Ash Grove*.

Years earlier on a family weekend trip we found all the verses to this old song and discovered an amazing, mystical verse that we did not know. The person in the song goes to the Ash Grove to have a peaceful, quiet time and the faces of his old friends, long since dead, appeared to him in the trees. It was as if my mother's spirit was traveling to that mystical place to find that sense of peace. But she didn't find peace there.

Suddenly I saw Jesus come to get her at the Ash Grove and away they flew, hand in hand to a different distant place. A group of people were gathering to welcome her to this place…people that I had never met but whom I recognized. My grandfather, her father, who died the year before I was born, was there to greet her. Her Aunt Pauline and her grandmother, Na, were there. They were all alive and so happy to see her. She was happy too. This was like a "video vision."

At my mother's memorial service the minister read from Isaiah 40…"Comfort, comfort my people Israel. Give her double for all her troubles… Jerusalem, herald of glad tidings, herald of glad tidings."(Isaiah 40:1)

I was stunned. My friend Harold brought me good news of peace to prepare me for my mother's passing. It was good news of hope and of eternal life. Harold, the herald angel… God sent a messenger to give me news to comfort me.

Several months later I saw Harold at church. He did not come to sit with me. After church I asked him if he remembered the time where he sat with me and gave me verses of good news. He did not remember. He had not been there.

What do I think happened? I think an angel dressed like Harold came to visit me, to bring me a message that I could not doubt, a message to give me peace. Harold was not sweetness and light. He was tall, big voiced and powerful, not what one would expect to see as an angel.

I wish I could say that these visions made my grieving easier and maybe they did. I was just aware of how much the loss of my mother in my life filled me with pain. I grieved for three years.

`My mother's older sister, Dorothy (we called her Dada) was in a nursing home suffering from emphysema. One day I took her my tape of angel stories and she loved the angel stories too. That Christmas my sisters and I created a little Christmas tree full of angel ornaments just for her. When she passed away I asked for that angel tree but it was nowhere to be found.

Harold was my second encounter with an angel. This time it wasn't just a vision in my head. I have heard several stories of people encountering someone they know bringing them peace or prayers only to find out that the real person was miles away at the time of the encounter. Angels can appear disguised as someone you know.

My father was in a nursing home when my mother died. My dad had been a general surgeon in Lexington, my home town. He operated in three different counties and three different hospitals. He practiced medicine for forty-nine and a half years. Why not fifty? Because of Alzheimer's disease. He was slowly declining in health due to

Alzheimer's disease. For a few years he knew he was losing his memory. His dad, a general family doctor, had suffered the same disease. One day my dad stopped talking about losing his memory. His awareness of his decline had been taken away by the disease. That was the only kindness the disease showed him. He had advanced beyond awareness.

At an Alzheimer's support group I learned that, if one has a slow onslaught of Alzheimer's, there will be a slow decline. If one has a quick onslaught, there will be a quick decline. Sadly, my dad's decline was slow.

When my mother's cancer was diagnosed, she knew she could not handle chemotherapy and caring for my dad. My parents were both very clear about wanting us to take them to nursing homes for care. They would have it no other way.

We found a home in Kansas City that had a special Alzheimer's unit and took my dad to stay there. It was a tragic day.

By the time my mother died, a year later, my father had no idea who we were talking about when we went to tell him the news. Sadly, as the weeks and months went by we lost my father, who he was and who he had been, piece by piece. In the early fall of 1992 my dad quit talking although he was up walking around and feeding himself. Then I got a call saying that he was in bed and losing ground quickly. My sisters and I gathered together by his bedside. He was unconscious. We spent a wonderful day running through memories, one after another. Friends stopped by to give quick hugs and sympathetic embraces. By the evening we realized that he could be in this place of suspended animation for days. My eldest sister,

Lucia, announced that she had a family to feed and was not going to stay. Shelly, my other sister, and I followed suit. We went home to our families.

After dinner, I decided to go back to spend some time alone with my dad. Nothing had changed. He was the same, unconscious and unaware. As the hour drew late, I decided that it was time to go but something was tugging at my spirit and I felt that I could not leave. Suddenly I realized that I had anointing oil in my purse and I could pray for my dad and anoint him with oil. If my dad had been awake, conscious and in his right mind I never would have done such a thing.

My dad was very skeptical about religious things and developed an animosity with the church when his favorite science teacher had been fired from his college for teaching evolution. He and his brothers and their dad were all men of science.... three doctors and a chemical engineer. My dad kept quiet about his bitterness towards the church when we were little so as not to influence our church attendance that my mom supervised. In his later years he overcame some of this upset. Occasionally he went to church with my mom and he was anything but enthusiastic about God and all that stuff.

So, I decided, in fact I was impressed by the Spirit to anoint him with oil. When I anointed him a bunch of angels appeared, standing in a long line extending from his bedside out beyond the walls of his room. I saw them with my spirit. As I said before, the first time I "saw" angels, it was like a pen and ink drawing. In contrast, this time, I sensed that the angels were dressed in robes of many colors, greens, golds, russets, browns, oranges, colors that seemed somehow familiar. I asked the angels if they would watch over my dad when I left. In a sort of quadraphonic "voice" they answered that, yes, they would watch over him and I could go home.

I felt released and free to leave and I said good-bye.

I slept well that night. In the morning I got the phone call that he had died.

My sisters and I gathered at my sister's house to go to Lexington to make funeral arrangements. It was a misty morning in October. As I drove to my sister's house, I drove up Lee Boulevard, a beautiful tree-lined street in Leawood, my town, a suburb of Kansas City, on the Kansas side of State Line. I felt the presence of the angels in the trees...and there they were... gold, greens, russets and oranges...the colors of the angel robes I saw by my dad's bed.

All the way to Lexington, as the mist parted, I could see the beautiful fall leaves and felt the presence of angels lining the road to my home town.

It was what the Celtic people call a "thin time". That is the time when the veil between heaven and earth is very thin and we can "see" to the other side.

When I was single and had my first teaching job out of college. My parents and sister, Lucia, came to visit to see if my living arrangements were acceptable and if my dad could do anything to fix up the house I was renting. My dad brought me a gift of a tool box with some tools in it...a screwdriver, pliers, a hammer, some screws and nails....the essential things. Tucked inside the tool box was a straw angel that had almost leaped into his hands at the hardware store. He knew I liked spiritual things way back then. He told me that he knew I was supposed to have it.

When I went home the day he died, I went to see that angel that he had given me so many years before. It was green with orange wings and a gold halo, the colors of the angels I had seen.

At the time, losing my mother to cancer and my father to Alzheimer's was excruciatingly painful. But it would not be worst struggle in my life. The worst was yet to come. The mystical experiences continued to sustain me, comfort me and bring healing to the many people for whom I prayed. Little did I know I was headed directly for a life and death struggle….and it would be my life and my death I would struggle for.

I am told I am going to Die

It is a strange phenomenon that, some of us only begin to truly live when we are told it is time for us to die. I lived with death knocking at my door for five and a half years. I lived five and a half years knowing how much I wanted to live. On October 13, 1997, I was diagnosed with primary pulmonary hypertension, called PPH for short. It is a disease in which the blood vessels in the lungs start to constrict, blocking the flow of blood through the lungs where it gets oxygenated. The pressure in the pulmonary artery rises to dangerous levels. The only symptoms of the disease were occasionally dizziness and shortness of breath. I had taken the diet medication Phen-fen and in return it gave me Primary Pulmonary Hypertension. Phen-fen, the lose-twemty-pounds-lose-your-life medicine.

With every breath I struggled to take, Death was there. Death stood right beside me. Anyone who has pulmonary hypertension knows this reality. It is a rare disease, a deadly disease, a life-sucking disease.

I was in a support group of people who had PPH. We all were on a medication that was delivered directly into our hearts by an infusion pump and a central line inserted through a hole in the chest. The medication was called Flolan. It was powerful, life-saving and brutal. We needed support to deal with the awful disease we were suffering through and to deal with the effects of this powerful, pain-inducing medication. The pump was a constant companion, 24-7, everyday, all day and night, for years.

Several of the people in my support group died before they could get life-saving lung transplants.... the only way out of PPH.. The saddest death was a 35 year old woman with a young child and a husband who didn't understand how bad this disease could be. She drove herself to Kansas City from her home town to get a heart catheterization. She died during the procedure. Her husband had to come to Kansas City get the car. Her pulmonary artery pressures were higher than mine, but not by much. I was walking on the edge of death.

One friend with PPH went to the hospital with wild heart palpitations. Being reassured by the doctor that everything was ok, her husband left her after she was settled down. An hour later he received a phone call from the hospital to say that his wife had died.

Denial was my friend. My sisters would tell you that. When they asked how I felt and I said, "Fine." They believed me. I believed me. The best way to deal with the stalking shadow of death is to pretend he isn't there, don't acknowledge his presence or his power. I denied it all very well.

The psalmist writes, Yea though I walk through the valley of the shadow of death, I will fear no evil for you are with me.

I trusted that God was with me (kind of)...the Lord is my shepherd. I just pretended that Death was not there. The valley of the shadow of death, even when you're in denial, is a very scary place to be.

Flolan was the medicine of choice for treating PPH, incredible powerful and unbelievably expensive, excruciatingly painful, tediously difficult to mix, an ever-present friend and foe all at once. It is a vasodilator. It opens the blood vessels wide so the blood can slip through more easily. The heart grows larger and larger as it tries to push the blood through the constricted blood vessels in the lungs. Every time the medicine opened my blood vessels up, I turned bright red all over. When I had to increase the level of medication the redness was constant and a friend would comfort me and say, "Today is not a good day for you to wear red."

Wearing red, being red, seeing red. It was a painful way to keep on living. The bottom of my feet ached, a side-effect. My jaw shot with sharp pain every time I took a bite of food, a side-effect. I had splitting headaches when those blood vessels opened up, a side-effect. Low cholesterol, too, was a side-effect. Yea! There was one good side effect! When the blood vessels opened so much, I teased that a truck could drive through them, and the cholesterol just moved on out. I lived with the fact that people stared at me when I was in public because of my bright red face and the pump that hung by my side.

Somehow I had been given the grace to learn from my disease. I believe that every struggle in life carries valuable lessons that create powerful transformation in our lives, if we will be open to it.

I didn't spend time asking "Why me?" Some people do and that's ok. It is part of the grieving process, but I just charged ahead, tried to have a positive attitude and keep my chin up and my body moving. My doctor insisted that I walk for exercise and keep working.

At church, when two or more people were standing talking, I asked for prayer. I got prayed for frequently, as much as I could. I feel God's presence when I am being prayed for. It is a very comforting experience. I had many words from the Spirit for my encouragement. I wish I could say that they sustained me but I would say it was fear that sustained me most. I was having a hard time really trusting the words I heard and the pictures I was given.

The church rallied to my support and offered to bring in food. I had a strange reaction. I refused. I didn't want that kind of help. I wanted to act as normal as possible. I wanted to grocery shop and cook as normal. I wanted to be as normal as possible

I had to have oxygen at night and when I exercised. The day the man brought my oxygen machine to the house, my husband Ken, our youngest daughter, Sarah, who was still in high school and living at home, and I sat in the living room and burst into tears-all three of us.. The oxygen machine had the name Invacare written all over it....the name of the company, I assume. I was being called an "Invalid" I was no longer valid, I was invalid. I was devastated. I was heart broken. We all were.

Our oldest daughter, Lucia, was away at college, but came home for a weekend to be with us. We tried to grasp what this turn of events would mean for us as a family.

My best defense in all this was to have a sense of humor as best I could. I named my oxygen machine "Darth Vader" because he sat in the kitchen at night breathing heavily in the corner, sounding just like the real Darth Vader.

There wasn't a lot to laugh about.

Funny things surface when a death sentence has been pronounced. I found that I had a basic wall around my heart that very few people got through and it was a wall of distrust toward people and God. I, who had great pictures and words of healing from the Spirit for others, could not let in the words and pictures that came forth for me. But I just did the best I could to keep moving forward.

My husband, Ken, was worth his weight in gold. As I had to drop pieces of my life that I could no longer handle, he just picked them up and helped me move forward. He remained encouraging and helpful. He went walking with me often for my exercise, even though we were moving at a snail's pace. He cleaned and did laundry, whatever it was that I could no longer do.

I kept on working, carrying my load at church.

As if being sick was not enough, the church where I am a minister became embroiled in a bitter battle and a split occurred. It was excruciatingly painful. People can become very hateful when arguing in the name of religion—who is right and who is wrong. I am grateful for the people that stayed with me through thick and thin. True friends are revealed when the going get rough. As in all our struggles in life, learning to forgive is an essential part of the transformative process.

In this painful time and dealing with a fatal illness I looked for angels but couldn't find any ….until one day, five years into my illness something amazing happened.

My doctor, Dr. Steven Stites, a pulmonologist who treated me for PPH, prepared me from the beginning, to get ready for a lung transplant. The medicine Flolan was meant to be a bridge medication that would keep me going until it was time for a lung transplant. I dreaded the transplant and hoped it would never have to be. The statistics of surviving the transplant or living after it were grim. 50% of the transplant survivors die within the first five years. It wasn't good news that a lung transplant is the only way out of the fatal disease Primary Pulmonary Hypertension. I was living with one foot in the grave and the other on a banana peel.

It is time for my Transplant

In September 2002 I mistakenly scheduled my check up with Dr. Stites on my birthday, September 5th. Ken went with me and our plan was to spend the whole day just messing around town trying several different eating venues for fun to celebrate. After my check-up Dr. Stites announced that it was time for me to go get my transplant. Ugh! Try as we might, we "celebrated" my birthday with heavy hearts, knowing that the inevitable surgery was starring us in the face.

I called Barnes-Jewish Hospital in St. Louis to schedule my final evaluation. Barnes is where I would have my surgery. It was there that I had been evaluated four years earlier and was accepted on the waiting list for a lung transplant. There were only 13 places in the country that perform lung transplants at that time. Barnes is one of the best. I was fortunate that it was so close to my home in Kansas City.

A friend's brother got his liver transplant at Barnes Hospital. He got a call in the morning and drove to St. Louis and got his new liver that afternoon. Lung transplant people are not so lucky.

Lungs are so delicate that a recipient must be present immediately when the lungs are ready. All the people waiting for lung transplants have to move to St. Louis and wait until their lungs show up. Moving away from home was part of the trauma of receiving a lung transplant.

Did I mention that I am a fear-based person? Everything scares me. Usually I am oblivious to my fear but it is always lying there underneath my cheerful façade ready to poke its ugly head up to bug me...to make me tense up. I was totally aware of how scared I was of having a transplant. One day, a couple of weeks after Dr. Stites told me it was time to go to St. Louis I was driving down the street when a vision popped into my mind.... while I was driving with my eyes wide open. It was a picture message from the Spirit. In the vision I saw the operating room at Barnes Hospital. It was cubically filled with golden light beings....angels, spirits of those who had died, and the spirits of people I loved who were still alive. They were gathered all around me during my surgery. The room was filled with golden pulsating healing light. I could feel the light. Peace came over me...a powerful, calming peace.

I thought, well, when I move to St. Louis, I'll get scared. I didn't.

When I get the call that my lungs were ready, I'll get scared. I didn't.

When I get to the hospital, I'll get scared. I didn't.

When I go to the operating room, I'll get scared. I didn't.

I never got scared through the whole process. The peace that came over me was always there. I think I would call it the peace that passes all understanding.

I believe that we all have a cloud of witnesses that surround us....golden light beings that love us and bring us peace.

Did I see the cloud of witnesses when I got to the operating room? No. But that doesn't mean they weren't there. I had seen them clearly and I knew they were filled with loving, healing light.

I went for my final evaluation in early December. I met the surgeon, Dr. Patterson. He asked if I felt better than I had in September or worse. For some reason I felt better. He said, "In that case, I'll let you go home for Christmas. If you had felt worse, I would ask you to stay."

I had to lie down in the car all the way to St. Louis and all the way home.

After my evaluation we started looking for an apartment. We found one but it felt kind of sketchy. Another one had too many stairs. Then we called Oak Wood Apartments. I explained my situation and the woman exclaimed, "You are going to have a lung transplant? Come on over. We had a man living here who got his transplant. This is good karma for us. Come on over!"

We arrived at the office and met another apartment manager who was equally enthusiastic about my transplant. This was kind of funny... kind of quirky. They really wanted me to stay there.   However they didn't have any first floor apartments available and I could no longer climb stairs. As we talked the manager said, "Actually we have another small apartment complex a few streets over but you may not like it. It is cheaper because it doesn't have a built in microwave."

As if I needed that!

"Strange," she said. "We have a first floor apartment available there and we usually always have the apartments rented even before they are empty. But this one is still available and they are painting it today. Do you want to go see it?"

So we saw it and it was perfect. It felt right. They understood I would not be back until January but agreed to hold it for me.

Lying down in the car on the way back to Kansas City, I remembered that I had asked God to help us find the right place for me to stay. I had heard the Spirit say, "I go to prepare a place for you." Sure enough, it was being prepared and painted just at the right time and it was for me.

Next came the Advent series that I was preaching at church that Christmas and then it was time to move to St. Louis. On the last Sunday of Advent I had a wonderful surprise waiting for me in church; my whole family came to hear my sermon and then the whole congregation gathered around me to lay hands on me and pray for me. It was such a beautiful send off. They all signed an anointed prayer cloth to accompany me.

Christmas was very special. Everyone gave me something for my move to St. Louis. Ken, my husband, gave me a travel book of St. Louis. My heart sank when I opened it. It was a piece of reality that I was leaving home.

In the evening, my sisters and their families gathered for our usual Christmas night dinner. Shelly and Lucia, my sisters, gave me an unexpected gift, the angel tree we had made for my aunt several years before. It had been lost until a woman cleaning my aunt's house, now my cousin's house, found the little Christmas tree tucked away in the attic. She remembered that someone in our family had wanted it. Now it was mine and the angels that bedecked the tree.would go with me to St. Louis. Lucia and Shelly also gave me a very special gift. It was in a pill bottle. On a long adding machine tape, wound up like a scroll inside the bottle, were the names of 350 people that Shelly and Lucia collected over the past months…. names of people who decided to become organ donors in my honor. What could I do but cry?

Early in January, Ken packed a truck with my belongings and some furniture, and I followed him, driving our car and we set out for St. Louis, four hours away. Miraculously I drove the whole way. In December I had hardly been able to sit up during the drive to St. Louis.

I checked in at the apartment complex and met the third of the three women managers. She, too, was so excited to have me staying in one of their apartments. I explained that Ken would be coming only on weekends until my surgery. She proclaimed, "If you need anything, ANYTHING you can call on my wonderful Luigi!"

He was her husband. She gave me his phone number.

Someone from the complex helped Ken move my furniture in. We made up the bed and he and our dog, Nana, disappeared down the driveway. I was left all alone.

The women managers at the apartment complex called me several times when the weather got bad to see if they could go grocery shopping for me or help me in any way. I think it is fair to say they were like three angels watching over me…. not mystical or magical, but just plain folks like all of us that, through acts of kindness and mercy, carry angelic love to others in a most ordinary yet holy way.

Several friends from Kansas City and from church came to visit me. I explored St. Louis in my car. Ken and Nana came to visit on weekends. Sarah came from her college, Marquette University and Lucia came from Boston where she was working and living.

I finished my training. Yes, we had to take two classes on how to manage life after a lung transplant. I was placed on the "pink card." It is the final step before getting the call that your lungs have arrived.

After six weeks of waiting, my women's group was coming to visit. They would take the train from St. Louis and I would pick them up. One by one, they had to cancel the trip for one reason or another. Finally, the only one left, Ronnie, came by all alone.

Now Ronnie has developed quite a gift of hearing from the Spirit. I had asked her to pray for others and she said she didn't know how. I said that it was easy. All she had to do was listen to the Spirit and tell the prayee what she heard. It was uncanny how well she did this. When she prayed for me, it was as if she were walking through my head listening to my worries and then answering them with words from the Sprit.

Knowing her incredible gift I asked her the most obvious question when she stepped off the train in St. Louis. "Did you bring a word from God?" I asked.

"Funny you would ask," she replied. "I've had this phrase rolling around in my head since the train left the station in Kansas City."

I could hardly stand the suspense, "What is it?" I had to know.

"Well, what I heard is 'You are at the end of your trail of tears'."

Wow! Wow! Of course, I knew that the correct way to handle such a statement is to hold it with an open hand and wait to see what would happen.

We went out to dinner. Spent time visiting and went to bed. In the morning we were having breakfast when I got a call from the hospital, the call I had been waiting for, the call I had been dreading.. My lungs had arrived.

I prepared to go for the surgery. I called Ken who headed to St. Louis. I called our daughters. Sarah started driving down from Milwaukee. Lucia made plans to come from Boston. I took a shower.

I drove Ronnie to the hospital where a friend met us and took her back to the train. Ken arrived and I went in for my surgery.

In the middle of the surgery the nurse brought my medicine pump out of the operating room. It had been my constant companion for five and a half years. My family gasped in fear. The nurse explained that I didn't need it anymore. I was breathing with my new lungs.

Five days later, I woke up from a medically induced coma. It seems that the surgeon had left me open for two days. My body was in such delicate condition it would have been too traumatic for the doctor to cut me open again if something went wrong. My enlarged heart was the size of a basketball. My liver, congested with fluid that my weak heart could not help pump out, spread across my abdomen.

I wish I could say that when I awoke it was a glorious and holy moment….the angels were singing and I was smiling, laughing and full of joy. But I would be lying.

`When I woke up I was suddenly aware of the nurse who was bringing me back to life and the male nurse that was standing at the door trying to flirt with my life-saving nurse. I was furious!

Now, no one can ever imagine what it is like to be as weak as I was. I felt like a way over-cooked noodle….just short of being total mush. I couldn't move. I couldn't talk because I'd been on a respirator for five days. But I could feel and I felt FURIOUS!

You never know when what you learned in high school would come in handy....real handy. All I had the strength to do was to roll my right hand over and raise my middle finger toward the guy in the doorway. I lay there, finger extended.

Finally the nurse saw what I was doing and said to the obtuse guy, "She's flipping you off. I think she wants you to leave."

Whew, she got the message.

The next seemingly unholy moment came after my first night in ICU when I was wide awake and unable to speak. The nurse, Paul, ignored me the whole night, preferring, I think, to spend time on his computer. I don't think he was updating files on that computer. I could see him returning to the computer after I would pull off my oxcimeter and make him respond to the corresponding alarm.

"Now you have to keep this on your finger, " Nurse Condescension would say. I was laughing inwardly knowing that an alarm sounded when I pulled it off and it was the ONLY way I could get his attention...first because I was cold, and next because my pain level had gone through the roof. Finally he noticed that I didn't have a call button so he went to find one. Half an hour later he returned having been totally unable to find a call button for me. Funny, the nurse the next morning found one right away.

My voice came back the next morning just in time to tell the doctor what I thought about Mr. Nurse. Whew, my family was listening totally appalled at my total diatribe full of swearing. I realized that it was kind of fun to swear so much, too.

I swore and I swore and I swore.

What I realized is that I always struggled to stand up for myself in life and now, even though I was waking from a coma, I stood up for myself very well.

And the burst of rage upon getting my voice back was probably a release of all the pent up anger I had not let myself feel for five and a half years of intense illness.

When I described the scene to Dr. Stites back in Kansas City he said "It was a holy moment. It was very holy."

Sometimes holy moments look different than one would expect.

Perhaps you are wondering why I would include this piece of my story. Partly I am doing it because it is true and partly to let you know that my "seeing" the amazing pictures I see and "seeing" angels like I do, doesn't not mean that I am anything but a regular person...with clay feet and all. I'm not "special" by any stretch of the imagination. I just have a passion for the things of God and the gifts of the Spirit and, other than that I am an ordinary human being.

So, back at Barnes Hospital, I woke up from my coma in pain, in weakness and ALIVE! Any shred of doubt that I had in God, any lack of trust or wall that stood between God and me was gone. ... and I believed and trusted in a whole new way.

The last time Ken delivered my rent check to the apartment manager's office, the women who had helped me so much were a little shocked. They thought Ken had found somebody new....he was with a new woman. Indeed he was with a new woman and that woman was still me. They did not even recognize me, the transformation was so amazing.

When I moved to St Louis in January I didn't know if I would be able to attend Sarah's college graduation. It was in May. Lucia and Ken assured me that, if I was still in St. Louis, they would be sure to make the graduation very special even if I could not be there.

In God's precious way, the timing was perfect. I finished the required three months of rehabilitation in respiratory therapy and exercise (an essential part of the lung transplant process) in the nick of time. I drove myself home to Kansas City (Leawood, Kansas, to be exact) on Thursday and we left for the graduation the very next day on Friday. All was well.

I Begin Painting

Back in Kansas City I reentered church life in full force. Our beautiful church building had been designed and built by Swedish immigrants and the kitchen had not been remodeled since 1938. I was on the committee that was dreaming and planning how to raise money to remodel the kitchen. We were a very small congregation….very small, very loving and not rich.

The idea occurred to me to paint some pictures of angels to try to sell to raise money for the remodeling. I checked out the idea with several people who were very encouraging.

I had always wanted to paint. My mother did decorative toll painting for years I .always wanted to try painting but never seemed to have the time or the energy. Before I went to St. Louis my friend Diane organized a painting group to teach us all how to watercolor. I made about 4 pictures and even sold two. Diane taught me how to relax and have fun with painting.

During rehab in St; Louis one of the rehab therapists, Yvonne, encouraged me to try painting. Yvonne brought in a volunteer who worked with the lung transplant rehab patients in painting. Yvonne is the woman I credit most with encouraging my art, right next to Diane's teaching. These things led me to decide to try painting angels to sell. I always thought it would be fun to paint the visions I had, too. Now was the time.

As I was contemplating these ideas one morning in quiet time, I heard the Spirit speak to me….

"There are no such things as old visions of angels to paint. I'll give you new visions to paint."

I objected, "That's fun Lord, but I don't know how to draw!"

I realized that I had a book of Picasso posters. So I dragged it out and studied. After looking at it I remember thinking, well, I could do something simple.

The next morning I was having my prayer and meditation time when- BAM....a vision of an angel appeared in my head. I took a piece of paper and drew the image. It was very simple and had very simple lines.

I put up a sign in the church fellowship hall...... the Angels Are Coming!

I got a big piece of watercolor paper and some acrylic paints (oils are hard on the lungs because of the turpentine with its fumes while acrylics are water-based) and I painted that first angel. I called him the Picasso Angel.

One after another the images came to my mind and I began to paint. Because I was still on a high does of prednisone and feeling high from the effect, I could paint from 5:00 am to midnight. I am sure I was high on the Spirit, too. The images kept coming and I kept painting.

I began to realize that, as I prayed for people, I would see images of their angels. Sometimes I would be standing next to someone and realize that I could sense the presence of their angels.

My style was very simple and people loved them. Also, the immune-suppressant medicine I was taking made my hands shake badly. You can see this in the paintings. It adds to the very primitive folk art style.

One friend commented that it was fun to see the angels but when you get your own angel painting, it is such a blessing.

I was in the middle of reading a Harry Potter book when this angel phenomenon occurred. I put the book down and never went back because this experience with angels was overwhelming.

I sold my first angel, the Picasso Angel for $300 and raised $5,000 for the kitchen remodeling fund.

I continue to paint angels, guardian angels, for people today.

Thank you for letting me share the personal story of what led me up to this wonderful experience of seeing and experiencing the presence of angels and painting what I see. If I just started telling about the angel experience, one would imagine that it was a wonderful yet frivolous experience. Instead, what is true about many mystical experiences, they are born after a painful and agonizing gestation. The beautiful gifts of the Spirit are transformed in human suffering.

Next, I will show you the images of the original angel paintings, captured on a CD by my photographer friend Paul Ingold. And I will try to express what these angels are conveying in their presence with us.

Be blessed by the angel stories and open your hearts and lives to see and experience the presence of angels in you own life.

In the following part of the book you will find pictures of the angels that appeared to me inmy spirit....which is how I see all visions. I drew the visions quickly then painted them on canvas board. I write about what they mean and what they are expressing.

The Picasso Angel

I sat down for my usual quiet time. This is a time early in the morning that I use to meditate or write in my journal, being open to what the Spirit is saying to me for the day. On this particular day, following my usual routine, a very strange and wonderful thing happened...a vision of an angel popped into my head. I quickly drew the simple, yet powerful image on a piece of white paper with black marker. Such simple lines conveyed such a powerful image. Freshly inspired to "so something simple" by looking at a book of posters by Picasso, I named this angel "Picasso Angel." His face is representative of what Picasso would do.

The angel is swooping toward me, hands outstretched as if he is announcing something. This angel is a herald angel, an angel bringing a message from God.

Picasso Angel has a many faceted green heart. Green is the color of the heart chakra. A chakra is an energy center described by eastern medicine. The chakras or energy centers emanate from the front of the spine, through the body toward the front of the person. Each chakra has a corresponding color.

In worship and prayer, I can feel the subtle change in my heart as the chakra begins to open up. This angel has come to open our hearts.

Faith and Hope, the Star-Faced Angels

Faith and Hope have stars for faces and they hold their hands in special ways. One hand is lying flat, palm opened to receive energy from the Spirit and the other hand is raised vertically, palm out, to send the energy to the person looking at the angel.

I did a teaching series at our church to tell the stories about the angels, showing the paintings. When he saw Faith and Hope, the star-faced angels, one man, Ken, declared that these were his angels. He purchased the picture. Later that year he became very ill with an infection in his spine. He entered a rehab hospital to heal. I took his painting to his room so that the angels could be there to inspire him.

One night, late, with the lights dimmed down, a nurse stood at the end of Ken's bed, asking if he needed anything. She started to shiver. Ken asked if she was cold. She said, "No, I am shivering because I feel as though I am being filled with faith and hope."

Ken asked if she had seen his picture. She had not but went over to look. He said, "Look at their names." She saw that they were

Faith and Hope. She placed her hand on the upraised hand and said that she could feel the Holy Spirit flowing into her from the picture.

May we all be filled with faith and hope every day.

Truth

"You shall know the truth and the truth shall set you free!" Jesus tells us.(John 832) It is so true!

One of my friends, Ronnie, has dedicated her life to finding the truth. This is her prayer... "May I be led into truth. May I find truth!"

Many of us are taught to be so nice that we hide the truth in the midst of terminal niceness. We are taught not to speak our truth because it might hurt someone's feelings or cause some discomfort. The truth gets buried so deeply that no one can find it.

Jesus came speaking the truth and got killed for it. He was protesting the religious system that had become a power play over and against the people. The truth of God's love and acceptance challenged the very existence of a system built on laws and rules so complicated that the average person could not live in much less succeed in. The truth of the message of God's love penetrates and exposes all pretenses.

Truth is powerful. Truth releases us from all that we have created religion to be. Truth sets us free!

Beloved I call You

©Marcia French
2003

Beloved I Call You

This powerful vision of the angel Beloved-I-Call-You came so clearly to me. She holds out her hand to us and her hand is filled with love as depicted by the multi-faceted heart on her hand.

Beloved is what God calls us. If we could know this for a fact our lives would totally change. We would be so full of God's love that heaven would come to earth and peace would reign.

Sadly, we have come to see God as an angry task master, demanding our obedience, doling out wrath in every direction. Jesus came to bring a new message....God is love. God watches and waits for us at every turn or even goes out into the world looking for us to return to his/her loving arms; to return to the home full of love that he/she has prepared. Unfortunately we, as Christians, have come to believe that we have to combine all aspects of the Hebrew scriptures (Old Testament), the teachings of Jesus and the opinions and rules of the Apostle Paul into one solid (albeit schizophrenic) religion. To me, the transforming truth that Christ brought is the only teaching to follow.

To discern the truth all we need to know is that Jesus, God and the Spirit all feel like love. We are God's beloved and that is the beginning and the end and the in between of the story.

Near to the Heart of God
©Marah Heisch
94

Near to the Heart of God

This angel is not just Near to the Heart of God, but is also extremely close to us...Near to Us. The image is like when you take a picture of yourself and you hold the camera close so that you just see a part of your face. So only a part of this angel is revealed...just a part of her face. The Heart of God is displayed on the foreground of the angel's fuchsia-colored wing. The Heart of God is many-faceted.

The more I talked about the angel, the more I realized I could not sell this angel. I could not let her out of my presence. I realized that this is my angel.

There is a hymn that I have loved since childhood back in the Presbyterian Church in Lexington, "Near to the Heart of God"….

There is a place of quiet rest near to the heart of God

A place where sin cannot molest near to the heart of God

O Jesus, blest redeemer, sent from the heart of God

Hold us who wait before thee, near
to the heart of God.

At Broadway Church the dance team created a dance to this hymn where the main dancer falls into the arms of God who is represented by both male and female dancers in white robes with golden sashes.

Where could there possibly be a better place than to be held in the arms of Mother/Father God, listening to the warm heartbeat of the Universe.

Peace Give I

This angel holds a person in her arms next to her heart. One might consider that the person is a baby, but it is a grown up. We all need love and nurture all of our lives even as adults. We are not usually bold enough to ask to be held but we all still need this kind of love.

Recently I got in touch with the fact that I was depressed as early as first grade. I think back to my wonderful, loving first grade teacher, Mrs. Linschied. She was so loving and patient with me. She would often share her orange drink with me. She sat in my desk with me helping me draw an elephant because my perfectionism was causing me great anxiety and frustration. I came from an intense home.

Most of us do not allow ourselves the vulnerability of saying we need such love, and this angel comes to give such love and nurture freely to this person...to this person's inner child.

Jesus said that we need to become like a child to enter the Kingdom of God. I believe that we need to get in touch with our inner child and that is where we will feel the presence of the loving, caring, essence of God who is Father and Mother to us always. This is where peace is found.

Power and Light

The energy of God and Spirit is a very subtle energy. Angels are made of subtle energy as well. The gift of prophecy or "spiritual vision" is a matter of being sensitive to the subtle energies of the spirit world. We can learn to open our spirits to see the other world.

The apostle Paul in the first letter to the Corinthians declares that this gift of prophecy should be sought by us all because it is used to build up the church.

This angel is called Power and Light because he/she transmits both energies to the willing subject. In the book of Revelation we read the description of an angel who has a face like lightening. That is what is being expressed here.

The angel's halo is an irregular spiked halo radiating the angel's energy through his/her crown chakra.

To see more clearly, we need the light of the Spirit that his angel brings. To live life more nearly in the flow of God's love, we need the gift of spiritual power.

Be open to receive the precious subtle energy of power and light for your life.

106

Power.
©Marcia Thia...

Power

This angel was painted for my co-pastor's son. It is called Power and represents the personal power within his spirit. I had an array of sixteen angels displayed in my dining room when my co-pastor came to visit with his granddaughter, his son's niece. I told her that her uncle's angel was depicted in one of the paintings. This young girl seems very spiritually sensitive. Out of the sixteen pictures she chose the correct one. She sees the possibility of this power in her uncle.

How do we recognize the power of the Spirit at work in people? One of the most spiritually powerful men I ever met seemed very meek and mild in his personality. Many people might call him "wimpy." When he prayed in the power of the Spirit in his spirit, all Heaven would break loose. The energy of love, peace, joy and healing poured out over the audience.

Sometimes the strongest spirit lives in the people who seem weak or wounded to us. The world of the Spirit works differently than ours. Some people have learned to access the power of the Spirit within them. Others, who seem so weak and incapable in our eyes, are carried along by the power of the Spirit alone.

In the mystery of this life our challenge is to see the Power of the Spirit and be blessed by the many packages in which it comes to us.

Michael

Michael is an Archangel that is seen as a protector. Here Michael's power is expressed in brilliant reds. His power is also expressed in his protection of the helpless.

Michael reminds me of my friend Rick who has a brother Mike. Mike is severely autistic and Downs Syndrome. Rick was 13 when Mike was born and always loved his special little brother. Mike has no speech, meaning he cannot talk. Rick and Mike's parents were instrumental in forming a school where children like Mike could go to a day school and boarding at night. This seemed fine for a long time. Rick would pick Mike up to stay with him on the weekends when he was transferred to KC from Washington, D.C. Eventually Rick found evidence of abuse and brought Mike home to live with him full time. Mike is truly among the most helpless of people.

Mike cannot dress himself, bathe himself, toilet himself and barely feed himself, shave or brush his teeth. Rick does all he can for Mike...all Mike can't do for himself and Rick loves him thoroughly. Rick's love and care for Mike have helped him live long and prosper to a much greater extent than possible had he stayed in the group home. Rick is like the angel Michael, protecting Mike in his helplessness. And Mike is like an angel to Rick, calling out his love and filling him with delight.

Knowing & Seeing
©Marcia Fleischman
2003

114

Seeing and Knowing

These twin angels represent a function of our growth in spiritual awareness and healing....seeing and knowing.

In order for us to grow spiritually we need to be healed and released from all denial. Denial might as well be my middle name. I am very good at it. In fact denial was very helpful in my disease as it allowed me to keep moving forward. It wasn't until two years after my lung transplant that I let myself know how truly bad I felt.

The medication that was pumped into my heart every thirty seconds was brutal. I had horrible headaches, my feet hurt and pain shot through my jaws every time I took a bite of food...no chewing gum for five and a half years.

I am good at denial in relationships in that I refuse to see what I consider negative things about people. It is easy to get hurt when you refuse to protect yourself from people's negative intentions.

So, Seeing and Knowing are essential attributes to living a life in truth and integrity. Honesty and truth live best in the presence of Knowing and Seeing. These strong and serious angels' hands are extended as they offer us the truth of what we need to see and the power of what we need to know.

Joy & Happiness

©Margie Fleischman
2003

118

Joy and Happiness

The dynamic duo, Joy and Happiness, are offering their gifts to the beholder. Joy, on the left, is winking at his adored person, and Happiness is smiling on him/her.

What could be more amazing than the fact that God who is love wants to fill each of us with Joy and Happiness. Those of us, who were brought up believing that God is angry and judgmental and full of wrath, missed that part about God being love. If God is love; can he/she turn angry, wrathful?

Does the ocean, which is made of water turn to stone sometimes? Does the sun above turn to darkness, rain or hail....No the ocean is always water, the sun is always radiating light and God is always love.

It is time to believe this good news. It is time to take it in.

Love makes all the difference!

These two angels are here to announce the good news....life is meant for Joy and Happiness!

May we all be released from the painful things that block out the love of God. May all of us find lives full of Joy and happiness!

God is winking at us!

122

Faith, Hope, and Love

"Faith, Hope and Love abide these three but the greatest of these is Love." The words of the apostle Paul ring so clearly and true in the great chapter on love, I Corinthians 13.

These three angels represent these great human capacities, faith, hope and love. Faith traverses all religions in its expression of the trust we feel when we know that the universe will bring about good for all of us in one way or another. Faith is the trust we feel when we see that some good comes out of even the worst tragedies Though we don't express these sentiments to those who have suffered the tragedy, we sit in silence, watching to see where the tragedy leads the people involved or the response by those who love and seek to alleviate the burden of loss or suffering.

Hope is a powerful ability of human existence. Hope is a belief that all things will work together for good somehow. Life will improve. Healing will happen. Somehow, some way we will grow in understanding in a trying situation. Somehow, some way we will be transformed by struggle and tragedy. Hope is the power that leads us forward in spite of the obvious obstacle, the overpowering pain, the loneliness of illness.

Love, the greatest of these, with her open, many-faceted heart is like the air we breathe, always there, always healing, always sure.

126

Mysterious Donor Angel

For a long time this angel has seemed mysterious to me. The image that came to me was quite clear, so I painted it. I think it was difficult for me to realize at the time that this is the angel that brought me my new lungs for my healing. The dark rose-colored wings actually appear to look very similar to a set of lungs.

While waiting for a life-saving lung transplant, it is difficult to know that someone is going to die so that you can live.

When I went to St. Louis for my evaluation I chanced to meet an "angel" that brought me the message I needed to hear. He was a middle-aged nurse taking care of me after my last evaluative heart catheterization. It was snowing and he was regretting that he couldn't be home to show his 2 year old daughter the snow. He said, "I know you probably think I am too old to have a 2 year old." In fact, I was just thinking about taking one breath at a time. But I played along and asked how that came to be. He told me that his daughter was really his granddaughter. His daughter had been killed in a car wreck. He met the woman who received her heart. I don't know how many lives she saved by donating her organs. I told him my misgivings. I'll never forget what he said…"People die anyway. If death can bring life to other people through organ donation, it is good to do. Don't be afraid."

Cloud of Witnesses

After my doctor told me that it was time for me to get a double lung transplant, I was so afraid. One day, while I was driving down the street, a vision popped into my head. I was used to visions, pictures that came to me as I was praying or meditating. But here a vision was coming to me with my eyes wide open and while I was driving. I knew it was a picture message from the Spirit.

In the image I saw the operating room where I would receive my lung transplant. It was full of golden light beings. I was aware that the beings included angels, the spirits of people that had died and the spirits of people still living that knew and loved me. I could feel the pulsating healing energy of golden light. The room was filled cubically and the ceiling of the room was gone as the golden light beings filled so much space!

The vision only lasted a couple of seconds, but the impact was enormous. Peace flooded my being. My heart was calmed and a peace that passes any of my understanding overcame all my fear.

I thought, "When I move to St. Louis, I'll be afraid." Nope! "When I get my call, I'll be afraid." Nope....never again was I afraid.

We all have such a cloud of witnesses surrounding us.

Cast Your Cares

Yvonne, the woman who encouraged me to begin painting, is a respiratory therapist at Barnes-Jewish Hospital in St. Louis, MO, where I received my lung transplant. Sometimes a person's greatest gift to others comes in a passion that transcends their profession. How would anyone put respiratory therapist, artist and mentor together? Yvonne does and her position has created a platform where she ministers to others and pulls creative energy right out of them and it helps in their healing process.

When Yvonne showed me her paintings I could not help but notice that her portraits showed such sadness. She confessed that this was true about who she is. Thus her guardian angel is one who asks her to cast all her cares upon her. Angels come to us as loving messengers and light beings that can absorb the pain we carry.

"Turn it over to God!" is a frequent encouragement from those spirit people who know best. What could be more delightful than a heavenly messenger who arrives to carry the pain, absorb the grief, enfolds the worrier with love and peace?

I went back to St. Louis for a week long treatment for rejection. Yvonne is now ensconced on the 13th floor where I was staying and we spent delightful time together. Her locks are longer now and her grief is gone.

Car Angels

I have heard several stories of car angels. A friend, Diane, was riding down the highway when an inner voice told her to slow down and change lanes. She obeyed. In a matter of minutes she came across a terrible accident that had just taken place. She realized that, had she not slowed down and changed lanes, she would have been involved in the wreck as well.

Another friend tells me that he carried concrete blocks around in his station wagon (was that awhile ago, or what!) for better traction in the snow. One day he had an overwhelming urge to take them out of the car. That afternoon while driving down the highway he was involved in a huge wreck. His car turned over several times, end over end. Wearing his seat belt saved his life and so did his removing the blocks. He realized in retrospect that had he not followed the strong inner prompting, those blocks would have rattled around in his flipping car and could have killed him.

We all pray that our car angels keep us safe. I think these angels are funny. They make me smile. I carried them in my car for several weeks until they went home with a friend who has a green car.

Just a reminder- when we hear that inner voice speaking and urging us to action, we must take it seriously. An angel may be speaking a message of protection.

Comfort Angel

This person is feeling very blue and the pale blue angel comes to comfort him. We are all in need of comfort. What do you do to comfort yourself?

When I became sick and was diagnosed with Primary Pulmonary Hypertension, I had to have a heart catheterization to accurately measure the pressure in my aortic artery. I came out from under the anesthetic too soon and was very much aware of the procedure I was in the midst of. The doctor assured me that the procedure was nearly finished. It was anxiety producing, to say the least. I realized I began rubbing my feet together. I had not done that since I was a little girl. Then I remembered that I used to rub my feet together while lying in bed at night just to comfort myself.

We all have favorite comfort foods...meatloaf and mashed potatoes, pot roast and carrots, ice cream, chicken and dumplings. How much better it would be to have an angel show up to hold us and nurture us.

In prayer and meditation we can close our eyes and feel the presences of the angels all around us. Sometimes it takes work and practice to get there. For most of us being held and comforted by a loving parent is a distance memory. Some therapist practice holding clients for its profound healing effects. Sit for a few moments and let an angel hold you now.

© 146 Marcia Fleischman

Computer Angel

Who doesn't need a computer angel? In this new age of changing technology, the angels are keeping up with us.

This little angel, with her hand solidly on the mouse, is surfing the net.

When my computer acts up, I need all the help I can get.

We don't usually think that the world of technology and science mingle with the realm of the mystical, especially with the angels. This does not present a problem to me. I believe that all knowledge comes from the Source…. the Creator. Even though new inventions come from the mind of humankind, it is interesting to see the sparks of insight that start people off in a creative, innovative direction. The intuitive part of us is also the part of us that is open to hearing or seeing the Spirit and receiving insight.

My aunt was in summer school studying higher mathematics which she taught in high school. One night her roommate in the dorm jumped out of bed to write something down. She had dreamed the answer to an impossible-to-solve formula. My aunt told her that she could possibly use the formula and answer for her Master's thesis. Her advisor in the program said rather that it could be used for her PhD thesis. Where did that dream come from…. synapses making contact or a flash of the presence of the Spirit?

Family of Angels

This was a commission of angels for a little boy who was just adopted from Guatemala into a family. The first son was also from Guatemala. This portrait of an angel family represents the people of the family. The parents, Tom and Michael, are on each side of the picture and the two little boys are the angels in the middle, one hovering above the other. They are all connected.

The group of family angels speaks of the blessings of God on this family. In these days it is not easy for families of gay couples to feel blessed by anyone let alone blessed by a church community or God.

In our community we find that all people are created in God's image and God's love knows no bounds.

Even the angels, especially the angels, bless families that are filled with love. The angels hover over the children. The scripture tells us that it is the angels of children that look at God all day. What a precious way to bless these little ones, by realizing that God holds them in such esteem.

Fri...d
154
©Marcia Stoughman
2023

Friend

This angel is my Friend. He holds out a heart full of love.

When my friend, Carol, saw this her question was, "Who is this friendly guy?" She picked up the energy that this angel is conveying.

We all need friends. As the old saying goes, we can't pick our family but we can pick our friends. The best saying about friends is...a friend is a friend for a reason, a season or a lifetime.

I have gained and lost a great number of friends over these years. A true friend is to be valued, loved and held in great esteem.

How amazing it is to have a spirit friend, like this angel, who remains a friend for eternity!

Guardians

These are the guardian angels that I saw guarding our daughter and her roommate who lived in New York City.

I have come to believe that each of us has at least one guardian angel or more. They represent the energy of God with us and around us, protecting us.

I remember reading a story of a woman who, one night in the middle of the night, was suddenly awakened and felt that she must pray for her daughter. She did.

She later found out that her daughter was walking home alone late that night from work. At the same time that her mother was praying, an unsavory man was lurking toward her, planning on doing her some harm. Suddenly he turned and walked away. Somehow it came to light that the reason he had turned away was that he saw two large men appear one on either side of the young woman, men of which she was unaware.

Sadly there are many stories of people who are not saved or protected, but I am reminded to ask for angel protectors and guardians whenever I can.

Little Blue Angel

This little blue guy represents the whimsy of God's angels. He is peaking out of the corner of the picture just to say "Hi" and to let us know he is there checking on us.

Since I really did not know how to draw, it has been fascinating in receiving these visions of angels at how easily we can express something in so few lines. This is the simplest of drawings, and yet is speaks so much of God's delightful presence, blue face and wing, green shirt, golden halo.

Do you ever think of God as one who comes to tickle our fancy...as one who is playful and joyful? This little angel comes to tell us about that part of God.

One of my favorite verses in scripture is: "Jesus, full of the Spirit, leaped for joy!"

So often we think of God as a being all serious, full of wrath and vengeance. I see God as love, the way Jesus taught. And, when God is full of love, God can be funny and playful, too.

I remember asking God for a porch to sit on in my first house that I would live in when

I was teaching in Bell City, MO, and living in Advance. Sure enough, I got my front porch! Only two people could sit on the top step of the porch. I could hear God laughing with delight at me on my porch.

Worship
162
©Marcia Fleishman '03

Power of Prayer Angel

This image of an angel praying shows the energy of the prayers rising from her like little sparks of lightening.

Do you believe that your prayers accomplish anything? Change anything? Heal anyone?

One dynamic story of prayer was of a woman who was in a car wreck. She died and her spirit was traveling above the wreckage. She saw the cars lined up behind her wreck and could hear the thoughts of the people. Some were upset that they would be late to work... many negative thoughts. But above one car she saw a swirl of light rising up from the car. She decided to go in the car to take a look. She found that the woman inside the car was praying for her...a complete stranger. She went out of the car and memorized the license plate number. She reentered her body and lived. After a long and painful recovery, she still remembered the plate number and looked up the person who had prayed for her, taking her a bouquet of flowers. (I wish I could give credit for this story, but I can't remember where I found it. Thanks to the author.)

Let this praying angel remind you that the energy and effect of our prayers are never lost but add light, life and even healing to the universe.

Praise

©Marcia Fleischman
2003

166

Praise and Worship

These angels are singing and worshipping God. They are light beings full of praise for the Creator. The interesting thing about this image is that it is focused more on the energy that rests in the middle of the group of angels rather than on the figures of the angels themselves.

One of the main functions of angles is praising and worshipping God. When I was studying to join the Presbyterian Church as a young girl, we studied the Westminster Catechism. We were asked a question to answer in front of the congregation. I was asked "What is the chief end of man." It was before the feminist movement and inclusive language were important. Now the question could read, "What is the chief end of men and women, or humankind?" The answer is "The chief end of humankind is to love God and enjoy God forever."

I have spent my whole life figuring out how to "enjoy" God. Now I would say it is in the act of worship. At Broadway Church we have been led to worship in a way that releases the presence of God's Spirit so that we can feel God's presence. It is a pleasure immeasurable to experience God in worship. These angels express the mystery that worship can be.

Projection Angel

What is it that this angel does not want to see? She has her hand over her eyes trying to keep something out of her view. Take a moment to look at her and write down what she is blocking out of her vision and her knowing.

As I showed this painting to different people, I realized that their answers were all different.....depression, greed, guilt, sexuality, sadness, anger. I realized the people were projecting on this angel the things about themselves that they did not want to see or deal with. This is a projection angel.

She has the power to dig up the issues that we have hidden within our souls or that we are hiding from in order to avoid dealing with them.

These are the things that are part of our shadow personality, the things hidden in our personal darkness.

When we pursue our own personal healing the Spirit performs what I call the "Spirit flush." Instead of flushing our issues down and out, the Spirit flushes our issues up... right up into our consciousness so that we can deal with them. We have to be willing to see our issues in order to know what to do with them .We must see and know them in order to be healed. Until we see and know them, they drive us in our thoughts and behaviors. Our shadow is a powerful motivator. Only in the presence of God's love are we able to see our wounds and fall into the healing arms of our precious Creator.

174

The Gift Angel

One delightful aspect of angels coming to us is that they bring us gifts. What would be the gift this angel brings you? Close your eyes and open your heart. Hear what your heart is telling you.

The work of the Spirit is healing. In Jesus' life we see that everywhere he went he healed people. One powerful story in John 5:6, Jesus asks the man, "Do you want to be healed?" It is a vital question for all of us.

Those who choose the path of healing are choosing the path of higher consciousness. To enter the healing journey we choose to open our eyes, see the issues or our lives, feel the pain, grieve and let go. It is a difficult and sacred journey. Not many choose it.

The work of the Spirit is to lead and support this healing journey. The Spirit, bearing the love of God directly to our wounded hearts, is the active agent of healing. When we empty out the sadness and pain of our lives, we need to fill up on love.

The angels also participate in this process, if we are open to receiving what they have to give. So the Gift Angel is bringing something important to help in each person's healing.

We need different things at different times. When you become aware that you need something, find this angel and see what she brings you.

Messenger

178

The Message Angel

This strange looking angel is a messenger. The angel displays a third eye in the middle of the forehead. In India women display a red dot placed on this most sacred of places. It represents the ability of spiritual human beings to perceive and "see" the things of the Spirit and the spirit world.

The Message angel is holding her open palms to her mouth. Her mouth is open as she breathes out the message of something she sees. This is called the gift of prophecy.

Many prophets are mentioned in the scriptures.... people that have the ability to hear from the Spirit or see in the spirit world and deliver the message that the Spirit is intending to send.

In the book of Acts the writer whom we assume to be John quotes

Jesus' coming as a time that was mentioned in the book of Joel:

And in the last days, says the Lord

I will pour out my spirit on all people

Your sons and daughters will prophesy

Your young men will see visions

Your old men will dream dreams

Even on your servants, men and women,

I will pour out my spirit

And they will prophesy. Acts 2:17

The presence and the power of the Spirit make hearing and receiving

Messages of God possible to the ordinary person.

Wisdom & Hope
Marcia Fleischman 2003

182

Wisdom and Hope

Wisdom and Hope were created for out daughter's roommate. She was stunned when she saw it. Hope was a most important experience in her life. She had a difficult childhood. When she went to college she decided to join a certain sorority because "HOPE" was in their motto.

When we are hurt, suffering, depressed, it is hope that carries us through the worst of times. It is hope that carries us beyond the pain to a more peaceful time. Hope is what helps us limping along through pain and illness to a better time, to a more joyful time.

Wisdom is not something we are born with. It comes to us as we walk through life. Life is meant for learning. When we learn from our struggles and our mistakes, we develop wisdom.

Wisdom is the capacity to see beyond difficulty to resolution and transformation.

Wouldn't you love to have Wisdom and Hope on your side?

186 Without Ceasing
©Marcia Fleischman
'03

Without Ceasing

Jesus tells us to "pray without ceasing."…….
This angel's mission it to pray without ceasing.
How can we understand what it means to pray
without ceasing? How can that be physically
possible?

We are used to defining prayer as "talking
to God." And talking to God for most of us
means speaking to God with our minds. There
are other ways to pray. We can sing to God.
We can meditate and let our heart energy
open to the presence of God.

The last way, opening our heart energy to God can become, through practice, a general state of being. Through the experiencing of the presence of God we can feel our single spirits connecting with the Spirit of God. This would be called "communing with God." This, I believe, is the essence of what it means to pray with out ceasing.

As we become more open to the Spirit through speaking and hearing the Spirit speak back we build a spirit bridge between God and us. That bridge then becomes a continued connector between God and us. This is what is called becoming one with God.

The messages of want and desire travel from our hearts and are always known to God. Sohpie Burnham in her book on prayer says. "I hardly pray anymore, and the things I want appear."

Luria's Angels
190
© Marcia Fleischman
2002

Lucia's Angels

Lucia is our oldest daughter. Her two guardian angels express two different energies that belong to her. The angel in the foreground is the angel Loving and Giving. She holds her hand out to give what is needed in each situation. She, like Lucia, likes her bling and wears a bracelet.

When she was a child Lucia said one day, "Life is so exciting, I just have to get back out there!" The angel dressed in pink is Lucia's energy of venturing out to explore the world. Her hand is open to receive what blessings and lessons come her way.

The visions of angels I received seem to express that the angels are very near us. One time a friend picked up my camera and inadvertently took his own picture. Because the camera was so close to his face, only part of his face was visible. Now the same thing happens with selfies. In these visions it is as if the angels are so close to us, we can only see part of their faces or part of their bodies. Such is the case with Lucia and Sarah's angels. Only part of them is exposed to view.

Sarah's Angel

This is our youngest daughter Sarah's angel...Joy. Like many of the original angel visions I saw, she stands with one hand flat and open to receive the love and energy of the Spirit. The other hand is open offering love and joy to the one she has come to love, Sarah.

Our guardian angels come to bring us love, peace and joy and whatever else we need.

Sarah is a happy and light-hearted person. This shows by the happy expression on her angel's face. She believes the best in most people but is very able to see what is not right. She is strong in personality and a very willing helper. Her guardian angel expresses many of the same qualities that Sarah possesses. She is strong and powerful yet fun and approachable.

Sarah is tall, just like her angel and of course, just like Sarah, she has to be wearing a little bling.

Serenity
198
© Marcia Fleischman
2003

Janie's Angel

When my friend Janie heard that I was painting angels for a fund-raiser at my church, she wanted to see one. This is the angel that she selected.... the praying angel.

Janie had the same disease I had, Primary Pulmonary Hypertension from taking the diet medicine Phen-Fen. We traveled the same road together toward our lung transplants. Sadly, Janie passed away just a few days after receiving her new lungs.

I loved Janie.

Do angles pray? Do they pray for us? Or are they the answer to our prayers?

Some people say that angles represent a part of us...a larger, light filled, best part of ourselves. Others see them as guardians or messengers from God.

If they are messengers to us, perhaps they are messengers to God on our behalf as well...all a part of the Devine Love and Energy that constantly surrounds us and lifts us up.

Paula's Angel
© Marcia Fleischman
2003

202

Paul's Angel

Paul is my co-pastor and has served Broadway Church for forty-four years. He has been the major encourager of my mystical experiences and my spiritual life. He is the person who taught me how to listen to the Spirit. He delivered a sermon one time called, "Hearing God." The brochure from that message is still available for the church office. That message started me on an amazing spiritual journey that has filled my soul with the presence of the living, loving God. I will always thank him.

This is a depiction of Paul with his guardian angel. The angel has very small hands that touch Paul's chest, near his heart chakra. The angel knows that Paul needs a very light and kind touch in order for him to open to the power and presence of the Spirit.

The angel's wings are wrapped gently around Paul's body in a loving, light embrace. Years ago I "saw" an angel with her wings wrapped around Paul during a sermon, just like in this picture. He announced the next week that he would be having part of a lung removed. The doctor suspected cancer. However, after the surgery it was found to be hystoplazmosis instead of cancer. We were all grateful.

The angel appeared ahead of time so we would know that Paul was in God's hands and being cared for.

Ivan's Angel

When I saw the vision of this angel I did not know whose angel it was. Ivan, a man at church, had a birthday party and suddenly, I realized that it was for him. I took it wrapped in birthday wrapping paper.

When he opened it, to my astonishment, he was wearing a shirt that had all of the colors in the painting. What affirmation! The Spirit had directed me in a very unknowing way to bless this person with an image of him with his guardian angel.

The angel stands behind Ivan with his hands on his shoulders showing that he is there to support and encourage and comfort his human charge.

Ivan's stands with his arms outstretched and his hands lifted palms up, to show his openness to the presence of the divine and his willingness to receive the blessings and messages that the angel is bringing.

Ivan's angel has "got his back" so to speak, a loving presence always there.

Peace
© Maria Fleischman
2003

Peace

In praying, this angel expresses one of the true aspects of connecting with God which is peace.

The more we truly connect with the Spirit of God, the more surely we will experience peace, peace in our inner core.

A long-time friend called recently to share that she would be having a medical procedure the next day. Although it was a routine procedure, she found herself in an extreme state of anxiety. I told her that I knew everything would be all right and assured her that I would be praying for her. Suddenly, as we were speaking, my spirit opened up and I "saw" a picture message for her....the operating room was full of angels. These angels were not of golden light, they were simply dressed in primary color robes....red, green, blue, orange. They were hovering over her and a very real presence of peace for her.

The day she got home from the hospital, I called to see how she was She replied that she had felt the prayers we were sending her. In the midst of her anxiety, peace came over her.

So the gift of God's presence with us is the feeling of peace. If all of our hearts would come to this sense of peace, inner peace that the Spirit brings, the world would be filled with peace. May it happen in our life time!

Wisparing Hope
214
©Marcia Haimsheen
2003

Whispering Hope

"Whispering hope, like the voice of an angel..." is the opening line of a hymn we sing at church. It is Jim's favorite hymn and we sing it for him. This is his guardian angel. He has his hand by his mouth to empower his whispering. Whispering Hope angel has a many faceted, multi-colored heart. The color combination reminds me of Superman's costume. Jim is a true super man, full of

God, faith and service. He, having been a micro-biologist, is also an accomplished handyman. Every Thursday he and his wife, Betty, spend four or five hours at the church. He patches and paints, fixes things and keeps the building from falling apart. Betty keeps the books of the church.

Jim lived through the WWII and raised two sons. He and Betty are very quiet pillars of the church who do not seek any recognition or thanks, but lovingly offer themselves in service. Through thick and thin at this ever-changing community of Jesus followers, Betty and Jim's faithfulness whispers hope to all of us.

Commune with Me

A song we sing at Broadway Church is called "Commune with Me":

Commune with me. Commune with Me.

Between the wings of the Cherubim, commune with me.

This angel, a Cherubim, wraps her wings around this person.

Many times in our spiritual or religious training we are taught that religion is a thinking exercise, a belief system...

.I believed this about God, while I was growing up. I learned this at church. I believe this about angels, Jesus, the Holy Spirit. That is why, for many people including myself, there is something missing. Since I was a child I sensed there was more to my religion than what I was being told. I now believe that the missing component is the EXPERIENCE OF GOD. God is meant to be experienced. If God is love, then we must be able to experience love and experience God.

Angels are meant to be experienced as well. This blue angel shows love and affection by holding this person. The person dressed in pink closes his eyes so he is not distracted by sight and can take in the love of the angel in a more powerful way.

Close your eyes now and open your heart to love. Imagine what it feels like to be enfolded in the wings of an angel.

222

In the Presence

These angels are standing in the presence of God. God is the light source in the center of the picture. God is the source of all life, light and energy. That source of light is so bright that the angels must cover their eyes.

It is a wonderful concept to see God as the Source of all things good, beautiful and right. We tend to see God as a limited source, a limiting energy. When we believe God to be wrathful, punishing and angry we want to limit our contact with Him. We live in a sense of limitation, believing God is denying us any pleasures or prosperity.

I remember a joke about God. God is in Heaven, looking over the balcony yelling at a person down below: "Hey, you down there. Are you having fun?"

"Yes, Lord!"

"Well cut it out!"

However God, the Source of all good is limitless. His/Her intentions for us are that we have what we truly want and that we have our highest good. "Ask and you will receive," Jesus challenges us. Jesus, knowing God, challenges us to find out how limitless our source is. God is so good that it hurts to look directly at Her/Him. The flow of God emanates throughout the world and the universe, carrying us forward into the light of infinite love.

Laughing Angels

These are the laughing angels I saw in a vision when I was very sick. I was at a Healing Prayer Team meeting in the home of a friend. I was in the midst of the best, most powerful pray-ers at church so, of course, I asked for them to pray for me. I was hoping for some comforting image of Jesus with me. Instead, while they prayed silently, I closed my eyes and suddenly "saw" Jesus standing off to my right front side, laughing heartily. Then he disappeared and the whole room and beyond was filled with angels all laughing and laughing. This made me laugh....that holy laughter.

This holy laughter has happened to me before in times when I have been overwhelmed by the presence of the Holy Spirit. In Toronto, Canada, a church was filled with laughter by the power of the Spirit. It was called the "Toronto Outpouring." It went on for months and people from all over the globe gathered to be blessed by this holy laughter. I have been blessed several times. This blessing is a feeling in the pit of my stomach that tickles and fills me with laughter, deep laughter.

That night it was Jesus and the angels that started my laughter. I was very sick and Jesus was laughing, the angels were laughing. That's because they all knew that everything is going to be all right. And that is true, through life and death; everything is going to be all right. We are in God.

To Be Continued...

Dedication

This book is dedicated to the memory of

Andrew Thomas Arnold
1988-2003

My lung donor, to the Arnolds, his family, who made my new life possible and to all organ donors and their families.

No greater love has anyone than that he lays down his life for his friends.
John 15:13

Also by Marcia Cope Fleischman

Angels Everywhere

Wild Woman Theology:
In the Arms of Loving Mother God

Broadway Church: The Musical

www.ingramcontent.com/pod-product-compliance
Lightning Source LLC
Chambersburg PA
CBHW041113120626
46547CB00019B/2684